MW01537150

OUT OF THE DUST

For My Parents
Louis and Evelyn Goldstein
My daughter, Maria
My granddaughters, Sarina & Juliette

Copyright © 2017 by Living Epistles Ministries
All rights reserved.
Published @ Long Island, NY December 2017

ISBN-13: 978-1545382530
ISBN-10: 1545382530

Alternate Translation Bible (ATB) ©
Sheila R. Vitale, Translator

No part of this book may be reproduced, in any form,
without written permission from the publisher.

Requests for permission to reproduce selections
from this book should be mailed to:

Living Epistles Ministries
Sheila R. Vitale
P O Box 562
Port Jefferson Station, NY 11776-0562 USA
(631) 331-1493

Living Epistles Ministries
~ Judeo-Christian Spiritual Philosophy ~
Sheila R. Vitale
Pastor, Teacher & Founder

Ministry Staff
Jesse Aldrich, Elder (McGregor, MN)
Sandra L. Aldrich, Elder (McGregor, MN)
Margaret Mobolaji-Lawal, Elder (Lagos, Nigeria)

Administrative Staff
Susan Panebianco, Office Manager

Technical Staff
Lape Mobolaji-Lawal, Database Administrator
Brooke Paige, MP3 & Software Specialist
June Eble, Shipping Manager

Ministry Illustrators
Cecilia H. Bryant (Oct. 18, 1921 – Oct. 23, 2013)
Fidelis Onwubueke

Music Staff
June Eble, Singer, Lyricist and Clarinetist
Don Gervais, Singer, Lyricist and Guitarist
Rita L. Rora, Singer, Lyricist and Guitarist

Table of Contents

The Alternate Translation Bible©

The Alternate Translation Bible **(ATB)** is an original translation of the Scripture.

Alternate Translation of the Old Testament©
Alternate Translation, Exodus, Chapter 32 (Crime of the Calf)©
Alternate Translation, Daniel, Chapter 8©
Alternate Translation, Daniel, Chapter 11©

Alternate Translation of the New Testament©
Alternate Translation, 2 Thessalonians, Chapter 2 (Sophia)©
Alternate Translation, 1st John, Chapter 5©
Alternate Translation, the Book of Colossians (To The Church At
    Colosse)
Alternate Translation, the Book of Corinthians, Chapter 11
    (Corinthian Confusion)
Alternate Translation, the Book of Jude (The Common
    Salvation)©

Alternate Translation of the Book of the Revelation of Jesus Christ
    to
St. John©
Traducción Alternada del Libro de Revelación de Jesucristo©

For Additional Information, please contact:

Living Epistles Ministries
Sheila R. Vitale
PO Box 562
Port Jefferson Station, NY 11776 USA

LIVING EPISTLES MINISTRIES

Sheila R. Vitale
Pastor, Teacher, Founder
PO Box 562
Port Jefferson Station, NY 11776 USA

OUT OF THE DUST

Is an Edited Transcript of LEM Message #004

OUT OF THE DUST

Transcribed and Edited For Clarity,
Continuity of Thought, and Punctuation by
The LEM Transcribing and Editing Team

Formatted As a Book by
The LEM Professional Administrators Staff

Out Of The Dust

TWO KINDS OF INCARNATIONS

The Express Will Of God

We are bringing forth a series of messages on the Gospel of the Kingdom. This is the message that will convert the hearts of the world. Please turn with me to the Book of John, Chapter 1, verses 12-13.

Jn 1:12-13

¹² BUT AS MANY AS RECEIVED HIM, TO THEM GAVE HE THE POWER TO BECOME THE SONS OF GOD, EVEN TO THEM THAT BELIEVE ON HIS NAME,

¹³ WHICH WERE BORN NOT OF BLOOD, NOR OF THE WILL OF THE FLESH, NOR OF THE WILL OF MAN, BUT OF GOD. **KJV**

The Scripture is saying that there are men who are ***not born of blood*** (the natural substance of the living soul that died), but of the substance of the Living God.

They were ***not born at the will of the flesh*** (as a result of sexual intercourse or the lust of the flesh), ***nor were they born by the will of man***, nor did fallen Adam, the living soul that died, rise up and say, ***I will return to my house. They were born at the express will of the Living God.***

Luke 11:24-26

²⁴ WHEN THE UNCLEAN SPIRIT IS GONE OUT OF A MAN, HE WALKETH THROUGH DRY PLACES, SEEKING REST; AND FINDING NONE, HE SAITH, ***I WILL RETURN UNTO MY HOUSE*** WHENCE I CAME OUT.

²⁵ AND WHEN HE COMETH, HE FINDETH IT SWEPT AND GARNISHED.

²⁶ THEN GOETH HE, AND TAKETH TO HIM SEVEN
OTHER SPIRITS MORE WICKED THAN HIMSELF; AND THEY
ENTER IN, AND DWELL THERE: AND THE LAST STATE OF
THAT MAN IS WORSE THAN THE FIRST. **KJV**

The Scripture tells us there are two kinds of men in the earth today: 1) those who are born in several different ways but, nevertheless, as a result of the soul realm's desire to incarnate, and 2) those who are born to manifest in the earth as a direct result of the will of the Living God. He sends forth His sons to manifest in the earth, and His sons are representatives of Him.

The Will Of Fallen Adam

We will zero in on how to recognize those people in the earth who have been born as a result of the will of the soul realm. We are told in Job that we existed in pure spirit form in the heavenlies with the Father before the earth was founded.

Job 38:7

⁷ WHEN THE MORNING STARS SANG TOGETHER, AND
ALL THE SONS OF GOD SHOUTED FOR JOY? **KJV**

The Scripture says that God knew us before we were born. Certain people, Jeremiah, for one, took on the flesh at the express will of the Father, to perform a function in this realm of appearance. When a son of God comes forth in the flesh, he comes forth in seed form. He appears to be a man of the earth, possibly, for many, many years, until Jesus Christ calls him forth. As the Scripture says, *I loved him, and called my son out of Egypt.*

Hosea 11:1

¹ WHEN ISRAEL WAS A CHILD, THEN I LOVED HIM,
AND CALLED MY SON OUT OF EGYPT. **KJV**

In a lot of churches people pass judgment on their brethren, saying, *You are of God, and you are not of God.* We do not know who God has chosen, because we cannot see into the hearts of men. Only Jesus Christ can see the heart of man. If somebody I knew fifteen years ago saw me preaching today, they would be amazed. I did not look like a son of God in any manner, shape or form at that time. I think all of us have this testimony.

We are to respect and honor all men and speak the truth to them. If they offend us, the Scripture tells us to rebuke them in truth, righteousness, and love, and to tell them they have offended us.

Eph 4:15

[15] BUT SPEAKING THE TRUTH IN LOVE, MAY GROW UP INTO HIM IN ALL THINGS, WHICH IS THE HEAD, EVEN CHRIST: **KJV**

We are not to go to someone outside of the Church and say, *I am incarnated at the will of the Father, and you are not*, because we do not know what God's plans are for that person.

JUDE 4-19, KING JAMES

Jude 4-13

⁴ THERE ARE CERTAIN MEN CREPT IN UNAWARES WHO WERE BEFORE OF OLD ORDAINED TO THIS CONDEMNATION, UNGODLY MEN TURNING THE GRACE OF GOD INTO LASCIVIOUSNESS, AND DENYING THE ONLY LORD GOD AND OUR LORD JESUS CHRIST.

⁵ I WILL, THEREFORE, PUT YOU IN REMEMBRANCE THOUGH YOU ONCE KNEW THIS, HOW THAT THE LORD HAVING SAVED THE PEOPLE OUT OF THE LAND OF EGYPT, AFTERWARDS DESTROYED THEM THAT BELIEVE NOT.

⁶ AND THE ANGELS WHICH KEPT NOT THERE FIRST ESTATE, BUT LEFT THEIR OWN HABITATIONS, HE HATH RESERVED IN EVERLASTING CHAINS UNTO DARKNESS, AND TO THE JUDGMENT OF THE GREAT DAY.

⁷ EVEN AS SODOM AND GOMORRAH AND THE CITIES ABOUT THEM IN LIKE MATTER, GIVING THEMSELVES OVER TO FORNICATION AND GOING AFTER STRANGE FLESH, ARE SET FORTH AS AN EXAMPLE, SUFFERING THE VENGEANCE OF ETERNAL FIRE,

⁸ LIKEWISE ALL THESE FILTHY DREAMERS DEFILE THE FLESH, DESPISE DOMINION, AND SPEAK EVIL OF DIGNITIES.

⁹ YET MICHAEL, THE ARCHANGEL, WHEN CONTENDING WITH THE DEVIL, WHO DISPUTED ABOUT THE BODY OF MOSES, DURST NOT BRING AGAINST HIM A RAILING ACCUSATION, BUT SAID, 'THE LORD REBUKE THEE.'

¹⁰ SPEAK EVIL OF THOSE THINGS WHICH THEY KNOW NOT, BUT WHAT THEY KNOW NATURALLY AS BRUTE BEASTS, IN THESE THINGS THEY CORRUPT THEMSELVES.

¹¹ WOE UNTO THEM, FOR THEY HAVE GONE IN THE WAY OF CAIN AND RAN GREEDILY AFTER THE ERROR OF

BALAAM FOR REWARD, AND PERISHED IN THE GAINSAYING OF KORAH.

12 THESE ARE SPOTS IN YOUR FEASTS OF CHARITY, WHEN THEY FEAST WITH YOU, FEEDING THEMSELVES WITHOUT FEAR. CLOUDS THEY ARE WITHOUT WATER, CARRIED ABOUT OF WINDS, TREES WHOSE FRUIT WITHERETH, WITHOUT FRUIT, TWICE DEAD, PLUCKED UP BY THE ROOT,

13 RAGING WAVES OF THE SEA FOAMING OUT THEIR OWN SHAME, WANDERING STARS FOR WHOM IS RESERVED THE BLACKNESS OF DARKNESS FOREVER. **KJV**

Duality

Everyone who has been incarnated at the express will of the Father has an element of the natural man in him. Even though the Lord God has willed our birth, the natural man is still a part of us, and the Christ in us is required by God to rise up and place the natural man underfoot and in servitude to Christ.

It is very difficult sometimes to tell the difference between someone who is incarnated at the will of the soul realm and someone who is incarnated at the will of the Living God. In a son of God, the battle continues until the natural man is swallowed up by the Christ within. The only person I know who has been processed to that point is Jesus Christ.

We live in an embattled state, and our own natural man is our worst enemy. He speaks his thoughts and intents right into our mind. He can put confusion on us by telling us the exact opposite of what God told us to do. Our greatest battle is with the natural man who comes from the soul realm of our own mind.

This message is important because it will bring people into the image of the Lord Jesus Christ. The Lord tells us to judge ourselves and not our brethren, and to get the mote out of our own eye, before we comment on and correct our brothers and sisters.

1 Cor 11:31

[31] FOR IF WE WOULD JUDGE OURSELVES, WE SHOULD NOT BE JUDGED. **KJV**

Matt 7:5

[5] THOU HYPOCRITE, FIRST CAST OUT THE BEAM OUT OF THINE OWN EYE; AND THEN SHALT THOU SEE CLEARLY TO CAST OUT THE MOTE OUT OF THY BROTHER'S EYE. **KJV**

CHARACTERISTICS OF THE NATURAL MAN

Filthy Dreamers

Jude 8

> ⁸ LIKEWISE ALSO THESE FILTHY DREAMERS DEFILE THE FLESH, DESPISE DOMINION, AND SPEAK EVIL OF DIGNITIES. **KJV**

The word *dreamer* indicates someone who is a vessel that ungodly spiritual power flows through. Man is a spiritual being: either the Spirit of God or the spirit of the *living soul that died* is manifesting through him.

We are conductors for spiritual life. You can be a dreamer and dream by the Spirit of God. If you dream by the Spirit of God you are called a prophet. If you bring forth the Word of the Lord into this realm of appearance because you have received a dream, you are a prophet of God, but there are those who dream by ungodly spiritual power. The prophet Jude calls them *filthy dreamers*. Do not listen to their dreams or what they say because they defile the flesh which reflects the power that exists in us.

We have learned that the flesh is made from the dust of the earth and that the earth is filled with creeping, crawling things. There is a great spiritual uncleanness in the earth. Nevertheless, we are told that we are sanctified by the presence of Jesus Christ in our members, because if the root be holy, so are the branches.

Rom 11:16

> ¹⁶ FOR IF THE FIRSTFRUIT BE HOLY, THE LUMP IS ALSO HOLY: AND IF THE ROOT BE HOLY, SO ARE THE BRANCHES. **KJV**

You can see the branches of a tree that are in the realm of appearance, but you cannot see the root that is underground.

If we have been incarnated at the express will of the Father and we have His substance within us, even though we sin and do things that are wrong, we are sanctified by the Christ dwelling within us.

This seed that we are born with must be activated. If God has not yet put His finger on you, saying, *I have known you from before the foundation of the earth, and it is time for you to come forth in My Spirit*, you may be living a very sinful life. You are not sanctified until you respond to that call, even if you are incarnated at the will of the Father.

The flesh is defiled by the evil spirits within it that bring forth ungodly behavior. We are sanctified or condemned by the spirit ruling in our flesh, or our mind. All of these spirits are in our mind. If we are serving God and purposing to live for Him, all of the creeping, crawling things in our flesh must come into submission to the Spirit of God. They are not there because we are evil or wicked; they are a part of our flesh nature, and God will prevent them from bringing death into our lives. Sin has the penalty of death associated with it. Jesus Christ is come so that we should live.

Despising Dominion

Jude 8

> [8] LIKEWISE ALSO THESE FILTHY DREAMERS DEFILE THE FLESH, DESPISE DOMINION, AND SPEAK EVIL OF DIGNITIES. **KJV**

These filthy dreamers despise dominion. The word *dominion* means *government, powers,* or *lordship*. The word *despise* means to *set aside*, *to neutralize*, and *to bring to naught* the ungodly powers in our mind that seek to set aside or neutralize the Christ within us. There are two men in our mind, Christ and Fallen Adam, and they are fighting for dominion of our vessel. They are fighting over who will rule our mind.

If Fallen Adam says, *I want you to fornicate*, and Christ says, *fornication is a sin*, who will win? What will your body do? What will your mind think? This battle is going on constantly. The words *despise dominion* mean that there is an unclean spiritual power

10

within us that seeks to put Christ under its feet and rule through our mind and body.

Only one spirit at a time can rule through a vessel, but the ruling spirit can change from second to second. It is a continuous battle. Only Fallen Adam or Christ can be on top at any given moment. This condition can flip back and forth from second to second.

That is why you must say to yourself, *I am tempted to do something ungodly, but I have the power to resist it, so I will not do it*. At that point, Jesus Christ takes the victory, but then the next day you go out and do it. What happened? There is a battle going on: one day, Christ is on top, and the next day, Fallen Adam is on top. If we throw ourselves on the mercy of God, and live in a state of repentance, no matter how many times we flip, Jesus Christ will sanctify us. We look forward to the day when we will no longer flip, but it is a process.

We are not expected to be walking in a 100% sinless lifestyle the minute we are saved. I flip all the time. Thank God for the Lord's mercy and delivering power in my life. It gets me out of trouble all the time, and I thank Him for it and glorify Him every day.

There is no condemnation in Christ Jesus if we manifest an unclean spirit or if we do something wrong or illegal. We throw ourselves on the mercy of the Lord, looking towards the day when He will rule and reign in our vessel. We look towards the day when Fallen Adam, the living soul that died, and everything he encompasses, will be in total submission to the indwelling Christ. When that happens in us, the government of God will have been fully established in our members.

Isa 9:6

> [6] FOR UNTO US A CHILD IS BORN, UNTO US A SON IS GIVEN: AND THE GOVERNMENT SHALL BE UPON HIS SHOULDER: AND HIS NAME SHALL BE CALLED WONDERFUL, COUNSELLOR, THE MIGHTY GOD, THE EVERLASTING FATHER, THE PRINCE OF PEACE. **KJV**

We are looking forward to being ruled by the government of God, because when that happens, we will stop sinning, and when we stop sinning, we will stop dying. That is our blessed hope, Christ in us, the hope of glory.

Col 1:27

²⁷ TO WHOM GOD WOULD MAKE KNOWN WHAT IS THE RICHES OF THE GLORY OF THIS MYSTERY AMONG THE GENTILES; WHICH IS CHRIST IN YOU, THE HOPE OF GLORY: **KJV**

Speaking Evil of Dignities

Jude 8

⁸ LIKEWISE ALSO THESE FILTHY DREAMERS DEFILE THE FLESH, DESPISE DOMINION, AND SPEAK EVIL OF DIGNITIES. **KJV**

The word *dignity* is the Greek word *doxa*, which is translated *glory, praise, and worship*. It is the word used to describe the Shekinah glory of the Lord Jesus Christ, the indwelling Christ within us.

These filthy dreamers speak evil of the Christ that is dwelling within us. That means they will do anything to keep Christ tread underfoot. If they fail, and Christ rules in our life, they will knock Him, they will deny Him, they will say He is not true. If we reach the point, spiritually, where Christ is ruling a large part of our life, these evil spirits in us will rise up and deny Him; they will speak evil of Him. Their first choice is to tread Him underfoot so that He should never show His nature through us. These evil spirits will fight to the death to lay hold of the property of the Holy One of God, which we are.

Rev 2:27

²⁷ AND HE SHALL RULE THEM WITH A ROD OF IRON; AS THE VESSELS OF A POTTER SHALL THEY BE BROKEN TO SHIVERS: EVEN AS I RECEIVED OF MY FATHER. **KJV**

He will be the head of every nation; every spirit within us that is not of God will be ruled by the Lordship of Jesus Christ.

Col 3:15

> ¹⁵ AND LET THE PEACE OF GOD RULE IN YOUR HEARTS, TO THE WHICH ALSO YE ARE CALLED IN ONE BODY; AND BE YE THANKFUL. **KJV**

Christ must rule. It will come to pass one way or another, because it is the will of God. No matter how many times we fall down, we get up, repent, brush ourselves off and keep on going. It will come to pass because it must.

The Body Of Moses

I became very excited when God showed me this Scripture in the Book of Jude.

Jude 9

> ⁹ YET MICHAEL THE ARCHANGEL, WHEN CONTENDING WITH THE DEVIL HE DISPUTED ABOUT THE BODY OF MOSES, DURST NOT BRING AGAINST HIM A RAILING ACCUSATION, BUT SAID, THE LORD REBUKE THEE. **KJV**

I have always heard this verse preached that Michael was contending with Satan over the dead body of Moses, but there are two distinctly different Greek words which describe a dead body and a live body. The Greek word for *body* in this Scripture is Strong's #4983, and it means *a live body*. The Strong's number for *a dead body* is #4430. They were fighting over *the live body* of Moses. What could that possibly mean? I looked up the word *Michael* in Strong's. The name *Michael* means *to lean towards, to bring near, to approach*, and in the Hebrew, it means *who is like God*.

Job 38:7

> ⁷ WHEN THE MORNING STARS SANG TOGETHER, AND ALL THE SONS OF GOD SHOUTED FOR JOY? **KJV**

Michael is a son of God who was with the Lord in the spirit realm. Michael was sown in the earth with the seed of man and the seed of beast. God promised that He would sow the seed of Israel in the earth with the seed of man and the seed of beast (man being the soul, and beast being the human body in which we live).

Jer 31:27

²⁷ BEHOLD, THE DAYS COME, SAITH THE LORD, THAT I WILL SOW THE HOUSE OF ISRAEL AND THE HOUSE OF JUDAH WITH THE SEED OF MAN, AND WITH THE SEED OF BEAST. **KJV**

The same Greek word translated *body* is used to describe the body of an animal and the body of a man. Human beings are animals. We live in an animal body. If the soul is absent (as may be the case with autistic people), that person is living on an animal level. Men existing on the soul realm have a body and a soul, but those who have been incarnated at the express will of the Father have the seed of Israel (the seed of Christ), as well.

The name *Michael* means *the one who is like God*. He was the representative of the seed of the Father, and he was contending with the Devil in a dispute over the live body of Moses. This is an example of the struggle that everyone who has been incarnated at the express will of the Father is experiencing.

Moses was an incarnated son of God. The seed of Christ was present in him at birth, and God gave that seed within Moses the name *Michael* so that we could understand what is happening today. Michael (the son of God who was in Moses) and the Devil (the soul realm that was in Moses) were struggling over who would manifest through the body, mind and mouth of Moses. That is what the struggle was about.

The Scripture says that Michael and the Devil *contended* for the body of Moses. The word *contend* means *to separate thoroughly, to withdraw from, to oppose* and *to discriminate.* When a son of God that is sown in the earth is born, he is joined to the flesh and to the soul realm. They are fused together as one. In the fullness of time Jesus Christ comes to an individual and says, *You may not know it, but My Son is in you. Come forth!* That is when the person receives the experience known as *salvation*.

14

God is calling you, and He has known you from before the foundation of the earth. He has been waiting for the proper moment to call you forth. From that day forward, He begins a separation process, because as long as the seed of Christ is fused to the seed of Fallen Adam, nothing but confusion will be manifesting in us.

Eph 5:26

²⁶ THAT HE MIGHT SANCTIFY AND CLEANSE IT WITH THE WASHING OF WATER BY THE WORD, **KJV**

This separation happens through the washing of the Word. It polarizes the thoughts of the carnal mind and the thoughts of Christ. If these thoughts are not polarized there would be a mixture, and Christ would never be on top because He is a part of every element. This process is preparing us for Christ to rise up in great power and put the soul realm under His feet. That is what was happening with Michael and the Devil.

Webster's definition of *to wash* means, *to pass water over or through, so as to carry off a material from the surface or interior, to move, to carry, to subject the action of water to separate valuable materials*.

God sowed His sons in the earth and is now bringing forth the Word of God to separate the seed of His life from the earth realm. There must be a separation. I have heard it preached that we are to come out of the world, but the coming out of the world is happening in our mind. We are to live in this world, but we are not to be a part of it. We are to think the thoughts of God in our mind.

Jn 17:14-16

¹⁴ I HAVE GIVEN THEM THY WORD; AND THE WORLD HATH HATED THEM, BECAUSE THEY ARE NOT OF THE WORLD, EVEN AS I AM NOT OF THE WORLD.

¹⁵ I PRAY NOT THAT THOU SHOULDEST TAKE THEM OUT OF THE WORLD, BUT THAT THOU SHOULDEST KEEP THEM FROM THE EVIL.

¹⁶ THEY ARE NOT OF THE WORLD, EVEN AS I AM NOT OF THE WORLD. **KJV**

To wash also means *to separate particles from a substance in water, to pass through a bath, to carry off.* That is what Michael, the son of God, was doing *within the mind* of the vessel that God called *Moses.*

Separation

We are separated through several processes:

We are separated through the Truth of God,

Jn 17:19

¹⁹ AND FOR THEIR SAKES I SANCTIFY MYSELF, THAT THEY ALSO MIGHT BE SANCTIFIED THROUGH THE TRUTH. **KJV**

By the faith of God,

Acts 26:18

¹⁸ TO OPEN THEIR EYES, AND TO TURN THEM FROM DARKNESS TO LIGHT, AND FROM THE POWER OF SATAN UNTO GOD, THAT THEY MAY RECEIVE FORGIVENESS OF SINS, AND INHERITANCE AMONG THEM WHICH ARE SANCTIFIED BY FAITH THAT IS IN ME. **KJV**

By the Holy Ghost,

Rom 15:16

¹⁶ THAT I SHOULD BE THE MINISTER OF JESUS CHRIST TO THE GENTILES, MINISTERING THE GOSPEL OF GOD, THAT THE OFFERING UP OF THE GENTILES MIGHT BE ACCEPTABLE, BEING SANCTIFIED BY THE HOLY GHOST. **KJV**

By Christ Jesus,

1 Cor 1:2

² UNTO THE CHURCH OF GOD WHICH IS AT CORINTH, TO THEM THAT ARE SANCTIFIED IN CHRIST JESUS, CALLED TO BE SAINTS, WITH ALL THAT IN EVERY PLACE CALL UPON THE NAME OF JESUS CHRIST OUR LORD, BOTH THEIR'S AND OUR'S: **KJV**

By the Spirit of God,

1 Cor 6:11

[11] AND SUCH WERE SOME OF YOU: BUT YE ARE WASHED, BUT YE ARE SANCTIFIED, BUT YE ARE JUSTIFIED IN THE NAME OF THE LORD JESUS, AND BY THE SPIRIT OF OUR GOD. **KJV**

By the Word of God,

1 Tim 4:5

[5] FOR IT IS SANCTIFIED BY THE WORD OF GOD AND PRAYER. **KJV**

By the New Covenant, and

Heb 10:29

[29] OF HOW MUCH SORER PUNISHMENT, SUPPOSE YE, SHALL HE BE THOUGHT WORTHY, WHO HATH TRODDEN UNDER FOOT THE SON OF GOD, AND HATH COUNTED THE BLOOD OF THE COVENANT, WHEREWITH HE WAS SANCTIFIED, AN UNHOLY THING, AND HATH DONE DESPITE UNTO THE SPIRIT OF GRACE? **KJV**

By God, the Father.

Jude 1

[1] JUDE, THE SERVANT OF JESUS CHRIST, AND BROTHER OF JAMES, TO THEM THAT ARE SANCTIFIED BY GOD THE FATHER, AND PRESERVED IN JESUS CHRIST, AND CALLED: **KJV**

The Lord uses these processes to separate us, make us whole, and free us from sin. When we come to the Lord and are cleansed by the washing of the Word, there is a separation of the mind of Fallen Adam from the mind of Christ. That is what was going on in the mind of Moses.

Contenders

Jude 9

⁹ YET MICHAEL THE ARCHANGEL, WHEN CONTENDING WITH THE DEVIL HE DISPUTED ABOUT THE BODY OF MOSES, DURST NOT BRING AGAINST HIM A RAILING ACCUSATION, BUT SAID, THE LORD REBUKE THEE. **KJV**

The word *contending* comes from the root word translated *judgment*. Throughout the New Testament, and in particular, the Book of Matthew, Jesus talks about the Day of Judgment, but He does *not* say that we will be thrown into hell and destroyed.

Matt 5:21

²¹ YE HAVE HEARD THAT IT WAS SAID OF THEM OF OLD TIME, THOU SHALT NOT KILL; AND WHOSOEVER SHALL KILL SHALL BE IN DANGER OF THE JUDGMENT: **KJV**

Judgment Day is the day you are separated from the natural man. After that, Christ goes on top, Fallen Adam goes underneath, and the government of God is established in your mind. That is the reality of the judgment of God. Jesus will do whatever He must do in order to bring us to that point, even if it is painful for us. We can make it through if we know that, at the end of the process, Jesus Christ will be ruling in our members, and we will receive eternal life. Judgment does not mean condemnation.

Disputers

Jude 9

⁹ YET MICHAEL THE ARCHANGEL, WHEN CONTENDING WITH THE DEVIL HE DISPUTED ABOUT THE BODY OF MOSES, DURST NOT BRING AGAINST HIM A RAILING ACCUSATION, BUT SAID, THE LORD REBUKE THEE. **KJV**

The word **dispute** means **to discuss, an argument, to reason with, to think differently about oneself; to argue from the Scripture, to separate in mind**. Michael was preaching the Word of God to the fallen Adamic side of Moses' nature.

When Jesus was in the wilderness with Satan, He used Scripture to answer every temptation. That is what Michael was doing to Moses' fallen Adamic (soul) nature. He was saying, **The Scripture says that you will come into submission to me, and I will rule in the earth of this vessel known as Moses. I will do the will of the Living God, and you will not stop me**. There was one point, however, when Moses failed. In the wilderness, God told him to speak to the rock, but he smote the rock instead.

Num 20:8-12

[8] TAKE THE ROD, AND GATHER THOU THE ASSEMBLY TOGETHER, THOU, AND AARON THY BROTHER, AND **SPEAK YE UNTO THE ROCK** BEFORE THEIR EYES; AND IT SHALL GIVE FORTH HIS WATER, AND THOU SHALT BRING FORTH TO THEM WATER OUT OF THE ROCK: SO THOU SHALT GIVE THE CONGREGATION AND THEIR BEASTS DRINK.

[9] AND MOSES TOOK THE ROD FROM BEFORE THE LORD, AS HE COMMANDED HIM.

[10] AND MOSES AND AARON GATHERED THE CONGREGATION TOGETHER BEFORE THE ROCK, AND HE SAID UNTO THEM, HEAR NOW, YE REBELS; MUST WE FETCH YOU WATER OUT OF THIS ROCK?

[11] AND MOSES LIFTED UP HIS HAND, AND WITH HIS ROD **HE SMOTE THE ROCK TWICE**: AND THE WATER CAME OUT ABUNDANTLY, AND THE CONGREGATION DRANK, AND THEIR BEASTS ALSO.

[12] AND THE LORD SPAKE UNTO MOSES AND AARON, BECAUSE YE BELIEVED ME NOT, TO SANCTIFY ME IN THE EYES OF THE CHILDREN OF ISRAEL, THEREFORE YE SHALL NOT BRING THIS CONGREGATION INTO THE LAND WHICH I HAVE GIVEN THEM. **KJV**

What happened? The fallen Adamic nature in Moses rose up, took dominion over Moses' Christ mind, and disobeyed God. As a result, Moses did not enter into the Promised Land.

God judges unrighteousness, but He brings you back; He does not condemn you. He brings you back, He brings you forward, and He brings you unto glory.

Many Accusers

Jude 9

9 YET MICHAEL THE ARCHANGEL, WHEN CONTENDING WITH THE DEVIL HE DISPUTED ABOUT THE BODY OF MOSES, DURST NOT BRING AGAINST HIM A RAILING ACCUSATION, BUT SAID, THE LORD REBUKE THEE. **KJV**

Michael, the archangel, was contending with the Devil over Moses' body. They were fighting over who's nature would manifest through Moses.

He dared not bring against him a railing accusation. The word *accusation* is the same Greek word that is translated *judgment*. The Greek word is *krisis*, and it means *decision, tribunal, especially divine law; condemnation, damnation, or judgment.*

The Scripture says Michael would dare not bring forth a railing accusation against the Devil within Moses because all judgment is given into the hands of the Lord Jesus Christ. We are not to condemn anyone, neither the natural man nor the believer who is manifesting the natural man. The Scripture calls us to judge ourselves and go on with God. Judgment happens later, when Jesus Christ is manifested in the earth. That is the job of the Son of God.

Jn 5:22

22 FOR THE FATHER JUDGETH NO MAN, BUT HATH COMMITTED ALL JUDGMENT UNTO THE SON: **KJV**

Michael would not dare judge the Devil within Moses, because God has committed all judgment unto the Son. Jesus said, *You are in danger of the judgment*.

<u>**Matt 5:21**</u>

²¹ YE HAVE HEARD THAT IT WAS SAID OF THEM OF
OLD TIME, THOU SHALT NOT KILL; AND WHOSOEVER
SHALL KILL SHALL BE IN DANGER OF THE JUDGMENT:
KJV

Judgment separates the soul realm from the Spirit of God within us. We are to judge ourselves by the power of God or submit ourselves to deliverance workers that the Lord has anointed to help us. Before we can help others, we must straighten ourselves out first.

Moses vs. Jesus Christ

We can contrast the experience that Michael had (in the vessel known as Moses), with what happened to Jesus Christ when He was tempted by Satan.

<u>**Mk 1:13**</u>

¹³ AND HE WAS THERE IN THE WILDERNESS FORTY
DAYS, TEMPTED OF SATAN; AND WAS WITH THE WILD
BEASTS; AND THE ANGELS MINISTERED UNTO HIM. **KJV**

Jesus had a different experience than Moses. Moses was not Christ. He was an incarnated son of God who was separated from his other self so that the Christ within could rule. Jesus, on the other hand, was the express incarnation of the Father. He was the offspring of the Spirit of God and the living soul.

<u>**Col 1:15**</u>

¹⁵ WHO IS THE IMAGE OF THE INVISIBLE GOD, THE
FIRSTBORN OF EVERY CREATURE: **KJV**

Jesus was the beginning of the creation of God. He was in a totally different category than Moses. In the temptation, ***Jesus was already separated and on top of Satan***, who was trying to convince Jesus to give up His position of authority. The separation had already taken place within Jesus. Satan knew that he was soon to be swallowed up by Jesus Christ and that he would no longer be able to live as an individual personality. Satan was trying to trick Jesus into giving up His position of authority, but Jesus Christ met every temptation with the Word of God.

We are told, in the Book of Romans, that the Lord God will bruise Satan under our feet.

<u>**Rom 16:20**</u>

²⁰ AND THE GOD OF PEACE SHALL BRUISE SATAN UNDER YOUR FEET SHORTLY. THE GRACE OF OUR LORD JESUS CHRIST BE WITH YOU. AMEN. **KJV**

Brute Beasts

<u>**Jude 10**</u>

¹⁰ BUT THESE SPEAK EVIL OF THOSE THINGS WHICH THEY KNOW NOT: BUT WHAT THEY KNOW NATURALLY, AS BRUTE BEASTS, IN THOSE THINGS THEY CORRUPT THEMSELVES. **KJV**

The people who are incarnated at the express will of the soul, or because the soul realm is prevailing in them, corrupt themselves. The Scripture uses the term *brute beasts* to describe people in whom the seed of God has not yet sprouted.

<u>**1 Cor 1:20**</u>

²⁰ WHERE IS THE WISE? WHERE IS THE SCRIBE? WHERE IS THE DISPUTER OF THIS WORLD? HATH NOT GOD MADE FOOLISH THE WISDOM OF THIS WORLD? **KJV**

They cannot understand spiritual things, so they rail against those who do. They do not know what they are talking about. They are not even on the same spiritual realm, so they are to be ignored. They are not allowed to damage us. If they try to harm us, we are to petition the Lord and pray against their efforts under the anointing.

We are not to do what Michael refused to do. If they are coming against us, we are not to rail against them from the same spiritual realm, or to meet them as a man. We are to seek God, ascend to a high spiritual realm, and respond to them from there. If we are not in a place in Christ where we can do this, we should go to the elder in Christ that the Lord directs us to.

Jas 5:14

¹⁴ IS ANY SICK AMONG YOU? LET HIM CALL FOR THE ELDERS OF THE CHURCH; AND LET THEM PRAY OVER HIM, ANOINTING HIM WITH OIL IN THE NAME OF THE LORD: **KJV**

Go to the elders of the Church, and they will pray for you, saith the Lord. An elder has the wisdom of God and sometimes has signs and wonders, ie, the ability to heal and cast out demons by the Spirit of God. You are not an elder because the Church gave you that title. I do not care what job you have, what you look like, or how old you are. I am looking for the witness of the Spirit of God. The work that He does in you confirms to me the wisdom that comes out of your mouth.

1 Cor 1:30

³⁰ BUT OF HIM ARE YE IN CHRIST JESUS, WHO OF GOD IS MADE UNTO US WISDOM, AND RIGHTEOUSNESS, AND SANCTIFICATION, AND REDEMPTION: **KJV**

The Scripture says that Christ Jesus is made unto us wisdom. We are looking for the wisdom of God. If we fight on the realm of the natural man, we will often be defeated.

Our motives have to be right. God does not require us to seek vengeance on anyone, because we cannot possibly know His plans for that person. God could be calling them forth at any time.

Rom 12:19

¹⁹ DEARLY BELOVED, AVENGE NOT YOURSELVES, BUT RATHER GIVE PLACE UNTO WRATH: FOR IT IS WRITTEN, VENGEANCE IS MINE; I WILL REPAY, SAITH THE LORD. **KJV**

All vengeance belongs to the Lord. We are to love our brother. However, they are not allowed to destroy us. If they are doing something that is hurting us, we must seek the Lord in righteousness and they will be stopped. Our motive must be a desire for the righteous judgment of God and not for vengeance. That person may have a problem we know nothing about, and we would be judging them unrighteously. When God judges somebody, He does it in a positive way which results in bringing that person closer to Him.

Rom 8:28

28 AND WE KNOW THAT ALL THINGS WORK TOGETHER FOR GOOD TO THEM THAT LOVE GOD, TO THEM WHO ARE THE CALLED ACCORDING TO HIS PURPOSE. **KJV**

1 Jn 4:19

19 WE LOVE HIM, BECAUSE HE FIRST LOVED US. **KJV**

All things work together for good for those who love the Lord. If you do not love the Lord, you will come to love Him, because *He loves you*. He loved us before we loved Him. He loves us all, and even if we are evil children, He will use every whack He gives us to bring us closer and closer to Him.

Jude 10

10 BUT THESE SPEAK EVIL OF THOSE THINGS WHICH THEY KNOW NOT: BUT WHAT THEY KNOW NATURALLY, AS BRUTE BEASTS, IN THOSE THINGS THEY CORRUPT THEMSELVES. **KJV**

In those things, they corrupt themselves. The word translated *corrupt* means *to move away from God*.

People that are manifesting the natural man, that are speaking against the sons of God, that do not know or understand what God is doing, are corrupt. What they do know is that you have something that they do not have, therefore, you must be wrong. When they attack you, they move further and further away from God.

The definition of a *brute beast* is *a man who acts without thinking*. We have all experienced this. I used to go into rages. I have been the recipient of a great deal of deliverance in this area. If somebody reminded me of something hurtful that someone else did to me many years ago, a rage would arise in me -- even though the person did not mean me any harm -- and I would say things that hurt their feelings. I ended up losing jobs (and worse) because I reacted as a brute beast. I did not stop to seek God as to the person's motives, or to think about what was happening in my life.

The Way Of Cain

Jude 11

¹¹ WOE UNTO THEM! FOR THEY HAVE GONE IN THE WAY OF CAIN, AND RAN GREEDILY AFTER THE ERROR OF BALAAM FOR REWARD, AND PERISHED IN THE GAINSAYING OF CORE. **KJV**

Jude 11 is talking about the condition of the man that has been incarnated at the express will of the soul realm. He will go in the way of Cain who was a murderer, and Balaam, who exercised spiritual power for personal gain. Korah denied the leadership that God gave Moses, and descended from his priestly office into the earth.

Isa 64:8

⁸ BUT NOW, O LORD, THOU ART OUR FATHER; WE ARE THE CLAY, AND THOU OUR POTTER; AND WE ALL ARE THE WORK OF THY HAND. **KJV**

The Scripture says that God is the potter and we are the clay. When a vessel is not coming forth the way God wants it to, He picks up His hand, and He goes *whack!* It goes back into the lump of clay, and He starts molding it all over again. That is what happened to Korah. He went back into the lump of clay.

Spots

Jude 12

¹² THESE ARE SPOTS IN YOUR FEASTS OF CHARITY, WHEN THEY FEAST WITH YOU, FEEDING THEMSELVES WITHOUT FEAR: CLOUDS THEY ARE WITHOUT WATER, CARRIED ABOUT OF WINDS; TREES WHOSE FRUIT WITHERETH, WITHOUT FRUIT, TWICE DEAD, PLUCKED UP BY THE ROOTS; **KJV**

Spots are hidden rocks. *Water* represents the realm of the Spirit of God. When I was newly saved someone in the church came over to me and gave me a witchcraft prophecy. She told me I had a spirit of witchcraft, which scared me half to death. Later I found out that I did have a spirit of witchcraft, but this woman hurt me because she gave me the prophecy in a wrong spirit.

If *God* sends someone to tell you that you have a spirit of witchcraft, it will result in your deliverance from that spirit. If someone comes to you in a spirit of condemnation, you will know that God did not send them. Unfortunately, many Christians do not understand this.

Jude 12 is talking about men that are incarnated at the express will of the living soul that died. They are hidden rocks; they are danger points in the realm of the Spirit of God.

They are hidden spots in your feasts of charity. The word *charity* is the Greek word *agape*, which means unconditional love. Agape love is the highest form of love that comes from the Living God. The word *feast* refers to *eating*. The true communion is the eating, partaking and sharing of the Word of God. When believers are gathered together, sharing the love of God and His Word, and all of a sudden, someone manifests an ungodly spirit, *that is the spot in your feast of charity.* It is the natural man coming forth to destroy what God is doing. He is eating at the table of the communion of the Living God, without fear.

Matt 22:12

> [12] AND HE SAITH UNTO HIM, FRIEND, HOW CAMEST THOU IN HITHER NOT HAVING A WEDDING GARMENT? AND HE WAS SPEECHLESS. **KJV**

In Matt 22:13, someone came into Jesus' wedding feast, and Jesus said, *What are you doing here without a wedding garment?* The wedding garment is the cover of the Lord Jesus Christ.

Clouds Without Water

Jude 12

> ¹² THESE ARE SPOTS IN YOUR FEASTS OF CHARITY, WHEN THEY FEAST WITH YOU, FEEDING THEMSELVES WITHOUT FEAR: CLOUDS THEY ARE WITHOUT WATER, CARRIED ABOUT OF WINDS; TREES WHOSE FRUIT WITHERETH, WITHOUT FRUIT, TWICE DEAD, PLUCKED UP BY THE ROOTS; **KJV**

Clouds appear to be solid, but they are made up of many particles. Man is a dust cloud. He is made of the dust of the earth, many particles of earth, fused together under great pressure, to give us the soul realm. Then God injects His Spirit into the vessel. If we are without the Spirit of God, we are only dust balls.

People who have been incarnated without the Spirit of God are *clouds without water*. They are *carried about of winds*. When an ungodly spiritual power comes to try them by offering spiritual knowledge or to spiritually manipulate them, they do not have the ability to discern whether it is God or an unclean spirit. They do not know that everything that is spiritual is not of God. That is a problem for people who move in a spirit of witchcraft. They think that everything supernatural is of God.

They are trees whose fruit withereth. They were born out of season, at a time when they could not produce fruit. Fallen Adam says, *I willed you into the earth*, but Jesus Christ says, *You are not fruit until I say, Come into the earth*.

Their fruit withereth, they are without fruit; they are barren. They are without hope of bearing fruit, because we can only bear fruit at the express will of the Lord Jesus Christ. Fallen Adam will be swallowed up by the Lord Jesus Christ, but the Lord permits him to bring people into this world.

Jude 4

> ⁴ FOR THERE ARE CERTAIN MEN CREPT IN UNAWARES, WHO WERE BEFORE OF OLD ORDAINED TO THIS CONDEMNATION, UNGODLY MEN, TURNING THE GRACE OF OUR GOD INTO LASCIVIOUSNESS, AND

DENYING THE ONLY LORD GOD, AND OUR LORD JESUS CHRIST. **KJV**

Jude 4 says that *certain men crept in unawares, who were before of old ordained to this condemnation*. These men will be used to try the sons of God. They will be used to tempt us, but they will not bring forth fruit. They have to go back into the clay pot to be formed at the express will of the Father.

They are twice dead. They are dead in the soul realm and in the spiritual realm. They are walking around like we are but without spiritual knowledge. They cannot tell the difference. Jesus says they are dead, they are *plucked up by the roots*. They will not continue.

Waves Of The Sea

Jude 13

¹³ RAGING WAVES OF THE SEA, FOAMING OUT THEIR OWN SHAME; WANDERING STARS, TO WHOM IS RESERVED THE BLACKNESS OF DARKNESS FOR EVER. **KJV**

The sea is a type of the living soul that died, and these men are raging and they are angry. We are called to peace in Jesus Christ. We are not supposed to be raging or to be subject to wild emotional passions. If you have the seed of Christ, the Spirit of God, you have the right to ask for deliverance in the name of the Lord Jesus Christ. You have the privilege of getting rid of raging passions which cause you to say and do things that (most of time) you do not even want to do, or that afterwards, you are sorry for doing.

They are *raging waves* of the soul realm, *foaming out their own shame*. They are ashamed because they do not have the cover of God. We are told in Genesis that Fallen Adam and Eve lost the cover of God and they became ashamed.

Gen 3:7

⁷ AND THE EYES OF THEM BOTH WERE OPENED, AND THEY KNEW THAT THEY WERE NAKED; AND THEY SEWED FIG LEAVES TOGETHER, AND MADE THEMSELVES APRONS. **KJV**

It does not matter how successful you are in the world or how much money you have. If you do not have the cover of Christ, *your spiritual condition is one of shame.*

Wandering Stars

Jude 13

¹³ RAGING WAVES OF THE SEA, FOAMING OUT THEIR OWN SHAME; WANDERING STARS, TO WHOM IS RESERVED THE BLACKNESS OF DARKNESS FOR EVER. **KJV**

A star represents *someone who exists in the heavenlies.* Today there are all kinds of people with all kinds of spiritual knowledge, but their spiritual knowledge is perverted. They deny Jesus Christ, and their knowledge is all twisted. That is why the Church world, in general, rejects spirituality. Many people have antichrist doctrine, but if we were to strip away the garbage, we would find that they have a lot of spiritual truth.

It is an error in the Church today that rejects everything that is different. The preachers are afraid that people will be deceived and get caught up into something ungodly. It is not true that the Church is the only source of spiritual truth. There is spiritual truth in every religion. It may be a kernel, but it is there, and if you are strong enough in Christ to not be polluted by the error, that kernel of truth can be a blessing to you. However, it is possible to be polluted. If you are young in the Lord, you should not go out looking for the truth in Buddhism or Hinduism, but that does not mean there is not a kernel of truth in those religions.

God has planted His spiritual knowledge throughout the earth, and now, in the end times, He is gathering up all these little bits of spiritual knowledge. He will *gather together in one all things in Christ*, and we will have the whole truth, and the truth will set us free. We need to have the whole truth, at which time Christ will swallow up Fallen Adam, and the government of God will rule in our mind. We will stop sinning, and we will stop dying.

Eph 1:10

> [10] THAT IN THE DISPENSATION OF THE FULNESS OF TIMES HE MIGHT GATHER TOGETHER IN ONE ALL THINGS IN CHRIST, BOTH WHICH ARE IN HEAVEN, AND WHICH ARE ON EARTH; EVEN IN HIM: **KJV**

Jn 8:32

> [32] AND YE SHALL KNOW THE TRUTH, AND THE TRUTH SHALL MAKE YOU FREE. **KJV**

Darkness

Jude 13

> [13] RAGING WAVES OF THE SEA, FOAMING OUT THEIR OWN SHAME; WANDERING STARS, TO WHOM IS RESERVED THE BLACKNESS OF DARKNESS FOR EVER. **KJV**

To whom is reserved the blackness of darkness forever. I did a word study on that phrase. It means that the men who are incarnated at the express will of Fallen Adam, not of the will of God, will be *kept in an unmarried state.* They will bring forth spiritual fruit for their lifetime upon the earth, but they will not bring forth spiritual fruit for the life of the ages. They will be kept in an unmarried state in the darkness of the realm of the soul.

The realm of the soul is darkness. Jesus Christ is light, and the realm of the Father God is light. *They will be kept in darkness, unable to spiritually reproduce Christ for the life of the ages.* That is the judgment of God.

Jn 8:12

> [12] THEN SPAKE JESUS AGAIN UNTO THEM, SAYING, I AM THE LIGHT OF THE WORLD: HE THAT FOLLOWETH ME SHALL NOT WALK IN DARKNESS, BUT SHALL HAVE THE LIGHT OF LIFE. **KJV**

Murmurers & Complainers

¹⁶ THESE ARE MURMURERS, COMPLAINERS, WALKING AFTER THEIR OWN LUSTS; AND THEIR MOUTH SPEAKETH GREAT SWELLING WORDS, HAVING MEN'S PERSONS IN ADMIRATION BECAUSE OF ADVANTAGE. **KJV**

In verse 16, we are given more characteristics of the natural man. I want to emphasize again that every believer on the face of the earth today, except Jesus Christ (as far as I know), is both Fallen Adam and Christ. We have elements of the natural man and Christ. If we do not have Christ, we are entirely the natural man, but we all have the potential to manifest every one of these ungodly characteristics. There is no condemnation in Christ Jesus. The condemnation on the unsaved man is simply that he does not have Christ.

Rom 8:1

¹ THERE IS THEREFORE NOW NO CONDEMNATION TO THEM WHICH ARE IN CHRIST JESUS, WHO WALK NOT AFTER THE FLESH, BUT AFTER THE SPIRIT. **KJV**

As soon as an unsaved man receives Christ, he becomes eligible to have the qualities of the natural man done away with. We are given the Spirit of God to bring all these qualities into submission to the Christ within us. God is giving us this information because He wants us to know the truth about our spiritual condition. The truth will set us free.

THE PARABLE OF THE SOWER

Matt 13:4-8

> ⁴ AND WHEN HE SOWED, SOME SEEDS FELL BY THE WAY SIDE, AND THE FOWLS CAME AND DEVOURED THEM UP:
>
> ⁵ SOME FELL UPON STONY PLACES, WHERE THEY HAD NOT MUCH EARTH: AND FORTHWITH THEY SPRUNG UP, BECAUSE THEY HAD NO DEEPNESS OF EARTH:
>
> ⁶ AND WHEN THE SUN WAS UP, THEY WERE SCORCHED; AND BECAUSE THEY HAD NO ROOT, THEY WITHERED AWAY.
>
> ⁷ AND SOME FELL AMONG THORNS; AND THE THORNS SPRUNG UP, AND CHOKED THEM:
>
> ⁸ BUT OTHER FELL INTO GOOD GROUND, AND BROUGHT FORTH FRUIT, SOME AN HUNDREDFOLD, SOME SIXTYFOLD, SOME THIRTYFOLD. **KJV**

Four Spiritual Conditions

Some people, even if they hear the Word of God, will not bring forth fruit. We will take a look at the four different spiritual conditions. According to the parable, there are three categories of men who *will not* bring forth fruit, and one category of men who *will* bring forth fruit.

Without Understanding

Matt 3:19

> ¹⁹ WHEN ANY ONE HEARETH THE WORD OF THE KINGDOM, AND UNDERSTANDETH IT NOT, THEN COMETH THE WICKED ONE, AND CATCHETH AWAY THAT WHICH WAS SOWN IN HIS HEART. THIS IS HE WHICH RECEIVED SEED BY THE WAY SIDE. **KJV**

These are people who did not receive the Word of God and have no understanding. I looked up the Greek word for *no understanding*, and it means *an empty mind*. They did not have the capacity to understand spiritual things.

We can only understand spiritual things by the wisdom of God, as He gives it to us. The natural man has no choice, which is why he is not condemned. God is not giving these men understanding, because they were not incarnated at the express will of the Father. It was not their time.

Some Spirituality

Matt 13:20-21

²⁰ BUT HE THAT RECEIVED THE SEED INTO STONY PLACES, THE SAME IS HE THAT HEARETH THE WORD, AND ANON WITH JOY RECEIVETH IT;

²¹ YET HATH HE NOT ROOT IN HIMSELF, BUT DURETH FOR A WHILE: FOR WHEN TRIBULATION OR PERSECUTION ARISETH BECAUSE OF THE WORD, BY AND BY HE IS OFFENDED. **KJV**

But he that receiveth seed into stony places, the same is he that hears the word, and with joy receives it. This is the natural man who has developed spiritually. When he hears the spiritual truth of God, he recognizes it as a spiritual truth and wants to believe it.

Yet, the Scripture says, *he hath not a root in himself, but endureth for a while: for when tribulation or persecution ariseth because of the word, by and by he is offended.*

He cannot hold onto it. When the Word of God (the seed) goes forth to bring forth Christ in us, we must have a spiritual element for it to fertilize. We must have the root of Christ which comes from the Father. When someone is incarnated or born at the express will of Fallen Adam, he is lacking the spiritual substance of the Father. Although he receives the Word gladly, it does not take root. There is nothing for it to hold on to, because God never said, *This is your time*.

Matt 13:22

²² HE ALSO THAT RECEIVED SEED AMONG THE THORNS IS HE THAT HEARETH THE WORD; AND THE CARE OF THIS WORLD, AND THE DECEITFULNESS OF RICHES, CHOKE THE WORD, AND HE BECOMETH UNFRUITFUL. **KJV**

Thorns are an element of the curse in the Book of Genesis.

Gen 3:18

¹⁸ THORNS ALSO AND THISTLES SHALL IT BRING FORTH TO THEE; AND THOU SHALT EAT THE HERB OF THE FIELD; **KJV**

The Lord told Fallen Adam that he would bring forth thorns and thistles.

We just talked about the natural man who had an element of spirituality built into him and recognized the Word of God as spiritual truth. Here we are talking about the natural man who has no spiritual development at all.

And the deceitfulness of riches choke the word, and he becomes unfruitful. He wants money and the things of this world. God does not necessarily want us to be in great need, but we cannot be overcomers and worship money, wealth, and the things of this world at the same time. Jesus says, *You cannot worship God and mammon*.

Matt 6:24

²⁴ NO MAN CAN SERVE TWO MASTERS: FOR EITHER HE WILL HATE THE ONE, AND LOVE THE OTHER; OR ELSE HE WILL HOLD TO THE ONE, AND DESPISE THE OTHER. YE CANNOT SERVE GOD AND MAMMON. **KJV**

God wants us to have our needs met. I do not believe poverty is holy, but we must put God first in our lives. We cannot do this if His seed is not in us. We must have the root of Jesus Christ to bring forth the new creation man, the offspring of the seed of the glorified Jesus Christ which is going forth right now.

The seed falls upon the root of Christ that is in our heart from birth. It fertilizes that root and brings forth the new creation, Christ in you. When Christ is born He rises up and starts to rule the nations that are within us. When Christ is ruling within us, we must overcome.

<u>Rev 2:26-27</u>

> 26 AND HE THAT OVERCOMETH, AND KEEPETH MY WORKS UNTO THE END, TO HIM WILL I GIVE POWER OVER THE NATIONS:
>
> 27 AND HE SHALL RULE THEM WITH A ROD OF IRON; AS THE VESSELS OF A POTTER SHALL THEY BE BROKEN TO SHIVERS: EVEN AS I RECEIVED OF MY FATHER. **KJV**

This is happening in our mind. As Christ comes forth, He must overtake the carnal mind of the natural man, bring it into total submission, and rule and reign over it.

He Who Hears & Understands

<u>Matt 13:23</u>

> 23 BUT HE THAT RECEIVED SEED INTO THE GOOD GROUND IS HE THAT HEARETH THE WORD, AND UNDERSTANDETH IT; WHICH ALSO BEARETH FRUIT, AND BRINGETH FORTH, SOME AN HUNDREDFOLD, SOME SIXTY, SOME THIRTY. **KJV**

He that hath received seed into the good ground is he that heareth the word, and understandeth it. We cannot understand the Word unless God gives us the understanding. That understanding rests in the root of Christ within us. We need to have something inherent within us that gives us the ability to understand.

ROOTS

Job 5:3-4

³ I HAVE SEEN THE FOOLISH TAKING ROOT: BUT SUDDENLY I CURSED HIS HABITATION.

⁴ HIS CHILDREN ARE FAR FROM SAFETY, AND THEY ARE CRUSHED IN THE GATE, NEITHER IS THERE ANY TO DELIVER THEM. **KJV**

I have seen the foolish taking root in the earth. The foolish are those without Christ. Fallen Adam is rising up and birthing people outside of the will of God.

Prov 12:3

³ A MAN SHALL NOT BE ESTABLISHED BY WICKEDNESS: BUT THE ROOT OF THE RIGHTEOUS SHALL NOT BE MOVED. **KJV**

There is *a root of the foolish* and *a root of the righteous*.

Isaiah talks about *a root of Jesse*. Christ came forth from the root of Jesse.

Isa 11:10

¹⁰ AND IN THAT DAY THERE SHALL BE A ROOT OF JESSE, WHICH SHALL STAND FOR AN ENSIGN OF THE PEOPLE; TO IT SHALL THE GENTILES SEEK: AND HIS REST SHALL BE GLORIOUS. **KJV**

Jesus Christ is the root *and* the offspring. When we are incarnated at the express will of the Father, we are incarnated as a spiritual female. The preached Word goes forth as the male element of the creation, fertilizes us, and brings forth the Christ within us.

One Creation In Christ

Jesus Christ is everything: He is the root, He is the female element, He is the male element and He is the offspring. He is bringing forth a creation whereby He can live and manifest in the flesh. This is the Gospel of the Kingdom.

God first brought forth a natural man. He did not lose control in the Garden; God is in control of everything. He brought forth a natural creation as part of the process which will result in the new creation. God intends to rule in this earth. Satan, the unconscious part of the carnal mind of Fallen Adam, will submit and be swallowed up by the Spirit of God. *He will be what he was intended to be from the beginning, the element of creation which gives it form.*

God is Spirit. Spirit has no form or shape, but God will live in the earth, and the natural man will be in total submission to Him. The creation will be joined to Him and He will rule. He will be all in all.

Right now we are both Christ and Fallen Adam. We will be one creation in Christ where Christ rules, and Satan, the unconscious part of the carnal mind of the natural man, will have no independent existence. The whole creation will manifest the nature of Christ. Satan cannot be independent of God. He must fulfill his function in the creation, which is to be a part of the form that the Spirit of God shines through.

In the soul realm, our flesh forms us. We are body, soul and spirit, but we will all be one in Christ. Jesus Christ is the only glorified man. All of His elements were joined.

Eph 2:14-15

[14] FOR HE IS OUR PEACE, WHO HATH MADE BOTH ONE, AND HATH BROKEN DOWN THE MIDDLE WALL OF PARTITION BETWEEN US;

[15] HAVING ABOLISHED IN HIS FLESH THE ENMITY, EVEN THE LAW OF COMMANDMENTS CONTAINED IN

ORDINANCES; FOR TO MAKE IN HIMSELF OF TWAIN ONE
NEW MAN, SO MAKING PEACE; **KJV**

Christ Jesus joined Himself to Satan, that same Satan who tried to tempt Him in the wilderness, which He resisted on every turn. That same Satan could no longer have an independent existence with which to tempt Jesus. Christ Jesus swallowed him up, they became one, and then Jesus Christ's body was glorified. He went up into the heavenlies. He has returned to the earth in the form of the Holy Spirit, and He is fertilizing all of us.

The same thing that happened to Jesus will happen to us. The Christ within us will be joined to (and swallow up) the carnal mind of our natural man, who will no longer be able to impulse evil thoughts towards us, or convince us to go astray, or to do anything wrong. Jesus Christ will rule, and we will ultimately be spiritual men.

Deliverance

The word *root,* in Webster's dictionary, means *source, the essential core, the part of an object which is attached to something else*.

Heb 6:19

> [19] WHICH HOPE WE HAVE AS AN ANCHOR OF THE SOUL, BOTH SURE AND STEDFAST, AND WHICH ENTERETH INTO THAT WITHIN THE VEIL; **KJV**

The root of Christ in us attaches us to the spiritual realm of God. He is the anchor of our soul. He is anchoring us to the spiritual realm of God and bringing forth the spiritual work of Jesus Christ in our mind.

First Christ must be separated from Fallen Adam. Then Fallen Adam must be brought into submission to Christ. The Lord Jesus Christ uses a process called *deliverance* to do this. It is the cleansing by the washing of the water with the Word. It is the separating of our thoughts into two distinct areas so that Christ can prevail, but what do we do with the bath water?

This vessel (which we are) is wrapped in flesh, and the part of us which is spirit is locked up inside. The purpose of the flesh is to give us form. Without it, our life substance would go pouring out.

Eph 5:26

26 THAT HE MIGHT SANCTIFY AND CLEANSE IT WITH THE WASHING OF WATER BY THE WORD, **KJV**

After our mind is cleansed and the thoughts of Christ separated from the thoughts of Fallen Adam, what do we do with the thoughts of Fallen Adam? In the Church today believers are pushing those thoughts to the back of their mind, and saying the thoughts are no longer there, but this is not true. They may be underfoot, but they are still there. Many people do not want deliverance because they feel that they are cleansed by the washing with the water of the Word.

God gave me a dream, which is an answer to the people who take that position. In the dream, the Lord showed me a wooden dresser. *Wood* typifies *man* in the Scripture. I was taking a bath in one of the drawers, and I was fishing around trying to find the plug to let the dirty water out because of the filth that had been washed away from me. I knew that I had been washed with the water of the Word, and that the filth had been separated from the Spirit of God within me, but there was no plug to let the filth out of the drawer. (There was no plug to get the separated filth out of my mind.)

We are able to push the filth to the back of our mind because of Jesus Christ's power. It can be underfoot, dormant, or bound up, but if it does not come out, there is always the danger of it rising up again. There was only one way, in the dream, that I could get the filth out. I had to take the drawer out of the dresser, turn it upside down and dump it out.

The Lord was saying to me, *There is no plug in your mind that will let out the filth that has been washed away*. Jesus Christ has only made one provision to remove the filth from our mind after it has been put underfoot, separated and overshadowed by Christ, and it is called *deliverance ministry*.

Deliverance ministry can be loud, and frightening to some, but deliverance washes away the evil thoughts from the unconscious and subconscious parts of our carnal mind. Demons are evil thoughts that have been birthed in our mind. Deliverance is the way to wash them out with the bath water. Even though you are separated from the filth, why would you want to walk around with repressed demons in your mind? You are a walking time bomb in that condition. When they come out, they scream and yell. Sometimes they make a lot of commotion. Sometimes they are very threatening, but there is nothing to be afraid of because Jesus Christ has everything under control.

Everybody who has the Spirit of God is a candidate for deliverance. First you must acknowledge that your thoughts or behavior have not been of God. Then you must repent. If you do not want to be constantly fighting off ungodly thoughts, and you long for the provision of God (which is the peace you receive in Christ Jesus when those thoughts are cast out of your mind), you can be delivered from them. If you desire it, God will surely meet your need.

PROPHECY

Yea, saith the Living God to His people, I have told thee, saith the Lord, that I shall be worshipped in Spirit and in Truth. Yea, saith God, the kingdoms of the earth deny this Word, saith the Lord. They have exalted themselves in high places. Yea, they are in My ministers, saith the Lord, and they stand in the pulpits across the nations, saith God, and they deny the truth, and they blaspheme My holy ones, saith the Lord, that would bring forth the Word that I have put in their hearts. Yea, saith God, I shall not tolerate this much longer, saith the Lord. Yea, indeed, even now, My judgment has gone forth to tear down this blasphemy, saith God, and not only the Church, but the whole world shall hear My Word, saith God. Yea, indeed, the Gospel of the Kingdom shall go forth, and in accordance with My Word, when the entire world has heard it, yea, that is the end. Glory to God! That is the end, saith the Lord, for I shall be all in all, and My Kingdom shall be established in the earth, saith the Lord. Yea, that is indeed the end of the systems of men, saith God, and the beginning of the establishment of the Kingdom of God. Yea, truth shall reign in the hearts of all men, and truly as the words that the prophet said, All shall be taught of God, saith the Lord. Yea, I am a righteous God, and I am a God of judgment, but I am not a God of destruction, saith the Lord. The truth of My nature shall be known, for I indeed have the power to resurrect whatever I destroy. Therefore, the definition of destruction in My Kingdom is not the definition of the word destruction in your kingdom. But I shall destroy every wickedness, and I shall destroy every evil, and I shall destroy every ungodly word and thought, but out of this shall come forth life, saith the Living God. Yea, My Kingdom and the life of My Son shall reign and rule across the earth. Hallelujah.

43

THE SEDUCTION OF EVE

Sheila R. Vitale

Living Epistles Ministries

EVIL CHILDREN

Sheila R. Vitale

Living Epistles Ministries

TABLE OF REFERENCES

ABOUT THE AUTHOR

SHEILA R. VITALE

Sheila R. Vitale is the Spiritual Leader, Founding Teacher and Pastor of *Living Epistles Ministries (LEM)*. Pastor Vitale has been expounding upon the Scripture through a unique Judeo-Christian lens for nearly three decades and has an international following. As head of the teaching ministries, she disseminates Judeo-Christian literature, both printed and online, to individuals around the world. Pastor Vitale also planned and organized the creation of Libraries of audio recordings of her teachings on Judeo-Christian Spiritual Philosophy, and distributed them across Europe, North America, Asia and Africa.

She also administers the organization's charitable giving. Under her direction, *Living Epistles Ministries* donates a significant percentage of its income to organizations that advocate for Judeo-Christian values, defend the United States Constitution and provide social services to individuals most in need.

In addition to managing the ministries, Pastor Vitale is an illustrator of spiritual principles, researcher, translator, social commentator, lecturer, movie, TV and theater critic, and author. She has given more than 1,000 *LEM* lectures that explain hundreds of spiritual principles, all of which may be purchased on CDs or as downloadable MP3s. In addition, beginning in the year 2013, Videos of Pastor Vitale's lectures became available for purchase on DVDs or downloadable MP4s. She has written more than 40 books based upon the Old and New Testaments, including *Not Without Blood*, *Salvation* and *The Three Israels*, as well as unique and esoteric translations of canonical Biblical texts such as *The Woman In The Well* and and *1 Corinthians, Chapter 11*.

LIVING EPISTLES MINISTRIES

Pastor Vitale began her training for ministry in 1978, and answered a divine call to begin teaching in the New York hamlet of Port Jefferson Station in 1987. The Lord spoke to her about teaching after she expressed her desire for a deeper and more spiritual understanding of the Bible. After that, under the heavy hand of the Lord Jesus Christ, she began to teach her own brand of Judeo-Christian Spiritual Philosophy that she calls *The Doctrine of Christ*. The Lord Jesus Christ named the work, *Living Epistles Ministries*.

Pastor Vitale prepared and delivered her first two formal messages entitled *The Truth About Witchcraft* and *The Seduction of Eve* in January and April of 1988. After that, she began preaching on a regular basis within the Office of Prophet and as a Teacher of Apostolic Doctrine, preparing weekly messages, including *Signs Of Apostleship* and *Lazarus & The Rich Man*. Pastor Vitale's unique, *Multi-Part Message Style* is seen in *LEM Serial Messages* such as, *A Place Teeming With Life* (9 Parts) and *Quantum Mechanics in Creation* (18 Parts). Pastor Vitale also analyzed the Greek text and preached extensively on the Book of Revelation in her early years, during which time she produced 197 distinct Message Parts under 29 distinct Message Titles that all deal with *The Book of Revelation*. The initial meetings of *Living Epistles Ministries* in 1987 were casual and spontaneous affairs. Formal, weekly meetings began in January of 1988, and gradually increased to two and then three times each week by the mid 1990's. She journeyed to Africa for the first time in 1992, where she was called to the office of Evangelist. After that she moved into the Office of Pastor.

Pastor Vitale travels internationally and domestically on ministry business, most recently promoting her signature accomplishment, *The Alternate Translation Bible,* an esoteric understanding of the Scripture which is not intended to replace traditional translations. Interest in the *LEM* message continues to grow today through the free video lectures on the LEM YouTube channel, the books that *Living Epistles Ministries* publishes, and the free written material that LEM distributes through its online reading room.

BEGINNINGS, INSPIRATION AND CALLING

Sheila Vitale was born into a Jewish family and began her spiritual journey as a child when her mother enrolled her as a student in an Orthodox Hebrew school. She also attended synagogue on Shabbat during that time, where she experienced the Spirit of God for the first time. Such a deep longing for God was stirred up in her that she wept. She was touched so profoundly that she became desperate to attend yeshiva (Jewish high school) but her parents could not afford the fees.

She became very ill around the age of 11 and has battled with chronic illness ever since. Her most recent struggle against premature death came in 1990, when she spent three months in the hospital before recovering and going on to resume teaching and managing *LEM*. Her illnesses led her to cry out to God, seeking a deeper understanding of what was happening to her.

Much later, as an adult, after years of searching, she, once again, experienced the Spirit that had brought her to tears, but this time it was in *Gospel Revivals Ministries*, a Pentecostal church where Deliverance Ministry was emphasized. She had desired a deeper understanding of Scripture since her early years, so she began to attend church regularly. She read at least one Chapter of the Bible every day but did not understand what she was reading. Scripture was difficult for her, and she struggled with the task. After about six months, however, while reading the Bible, she saw a vision of the angel with the little book described in Chapter 10 of the Book of Revelation, verse 8. She began to understand the Bible after that, but several more years had to pass before she began to receive Revelation knowledge of the Scripture.

Sheila Vitale studied the Bible and Deliverance Ministry for about seven years under the teaching of *Charles Holzhauser*, the Pastor of *Gospel Revivals Ministries*, in Mount Sinai, NY. Sometimes she attended as many as five teaching services each week, as well as studying for endless hours to gain key insight into her faith. She also edited *Pastor Holzhauser's* books during that time. After that, she studied independently under the influence and direction of the Holy Spirit, before founding *Living Epistles Ministries*.

WRITINGS AND WORK TODAY

Sheila Vitale's signature work is the three volumes of *The Alternate Translation Bible*: *The Alternate Translation Of The Old Testament*, *The Alternate Translation of the New Testament* and *The Alternate Translation of the Book of Revelation*. The Alternate Translation Bible is an esoteric translation of the Scripture and is not intended to replace traditional translations. *The Book of Revelation* and several other books that Pastor Vitale has written have been translated into Spanish.

LEM books are displayed on the official LEM website (LivingEpistles.org) and Paperback and digital versions of LEM books may be purchased at Amazon.com, BarnesandNoble.com, and Google Bools. She also has an Amazon *Author's Central* Website which displays all of her books, a short bio and several photographs of her.

She has also written extensive reviews for movies, TV shows and plays which are based upon spiritual principles, such as *The Matrix*, *The Edge of Tomorrow* and *Wicked*. Pastor Vitale also analyzes modern Social Trends in view of the Scripture and, in that vein, reviews media that deals with Family and Culture, such as the TV series, *The Sopranos*. She also writes for the *Blog* on the *LEM* website, where a detailed review of radio talk show host Alex Jones' interview of Louis Farrakhan is posted. She has also delivered hundreds of messages, many of which have been transcribed. Message transcripts may be read free of charge on the *Living Epistles* website.

Short, focused video messages by Sheila Vitale, averaging 15 minutes each are also available on a second *LEM YouTube* channel called, *Short Clips by Sheila R. Vitale.*

PASTOR VITALE TODAY

Sheila Vitale serves a range of ecclesiastical, educational, and administrative functions from her headquarters in Selden, New York. Operating in the Offices of Evangelist, Prophet, Teacher of Apostolic Doctrine and Pastor, she continues delivering her powerful messages on a range of topics from movie reviews and social commentaries to doctrinal error, esoteric interpretations of the Scripture, Judeo-Christian Spiritual Foundations, Spiritual Philosophy, Salvation, Faith, Truth, Judgment, and Spiritual Warfare.

She has dedicated her life to studying and teaching Judeo-Christian spiritual principles, and continues to focus daily on studying, teaching and writing. In February of 2016, she joined other teachers to dedicate a Living Epistles Ministries Building in Gray Court, South Carolina.

She is also a philanthropic individual who supports numerous charitable organizations, including *Feed the Children*, *Judicial Watch*, *World Vision*, *Lighthouse Mission*, and *The International Fellowship of Christians and Jews*. She also helps local groups such as the *Terryville Fire Department*. In her spare time, Pastor Vitale enjoys watching movies, attending plays and partaking of cuisines from different cultures. An avid traveler, she has visited numerous countries in Europe and Africa as well as many cities in the United States.

Living Epistles Ministries
Sheila R. Vitale
Pastor, Teacher & Founder
Judeo-Christian Spiritual Philosophy
PO Box 562, Port Jefferson Station, New York 11776, USA
LivingEpistles.org
or
Books@LivingEpistles.org

23550977R00040

Made in the USA
San Bernardino, CA
27 January 2019